# French Tangos for Accordion

*by Gary Dahl*

Online Audio www.melbay.com/96927BCDEB

## Audio Contents

| | | | | | |
|---|---|---|---|---|---|
| 1 | Joue Contre Joue [2:01] | 13 | Maïa [2:21] | 25 | Ma Rose D'Alsace [1:58] |
| 2 | Cara Al Cielo [1:15] | 14 | Téléphonez-Moi Chérie [3:55] | 26 | Tango – Maison [2:36] |
| 3 | El Choclo [1:58] | 15 | Si Tu Reviens [1:19] | 27 | Le Tango Argentin [1:15] |
| 4 | J'ai Pleuré Sur Tes Pas [1:49] | 16 | Sacré Tango [1:37] | 28 | Un Tango D'autrefois [1:53] |
| 5 | Tango Du Souvenir [3:37] | 17 | Le Tango De La Mélancolie [1:42] | 29 | Baisse un peu L'Abat-Jour [1:32] |
| 6 | Soir de Pluie [1:57] | 18 | Tango Pour Madame [1:45] | 30 | Une Simple Carte Postale [1:17] |
| 7 | As De Copas [2:39] | 19 | Simple Tango [2:49] | 31 | Aïe, Aïe, Tango [1:58] |
| 8 | J'ai Gardé Ta Photo [1:07] | 20 | Ta Jalousie [1:09] | 32 | Pour Sûr [1:09] |
| 9 | La Paloma [2:00] | 21 | Le Tango Des Mariniers [1:54] | 33 | Passion Madrileñe [1:39] |
| 10 | Tango Gitano [2:42] | 22 | Sensual (Tango) [1:39] | 34 | Le Temps D'un Tango [1:22] |
| 11 | Tangorama [1:21] | 23 | Tango – Musette [2:47] | 35 | Tango Fleur Bleue [2:44] |
| 12 | Insaisissable [2:18] | 24 | La Madone D'amour [2:23 | | |

**Due to time constraints, some repeats have been omitted.**

1 2 3 4 5 6 7 8 9 0



*Visit us on the Web at http://www.melbay.com — E-mail us at email@melbay.com*

# Contents

# Foreword

THE TANGO: A ballroom dance of Latin American origin characterized by long pauses and stylized body positions. The musical form of tango was later adopted by other countries; primarily France, Spain and Italy. Many prominent composers have utilized this form in a wide variety of compositions.

*French Tangos For Accordion* has been skillfully arranged from piano and orchestra scores by Gary Dahl with extra compositional writing to take advantage of the accordion's orchestral capabilities. The arranging uses both the Latin American and Spanish rhythmic styles. This music was published from the late 1930s to 1970. The pieces are very romantic, utilizing rich and sometimes avant garde harmonies supporting emotional melodies. The arrangements are written orchestrally to fit the various timbres and unique capabilities of today's modern accordion.

Gary Dahl is certified by the American Accordionist's Association, Northwest Accordion Teacher's Association and received a BA degree from the University of Washington with a minor in music theory/harmony. Mr. Dahl's students have been consistent winners in National/State competitions and many have achieved professional status. The Gary Dahl Trio plus vocalist performed regularly at private clubs, hotels and lounges. Mr. Dahl studied with Joe Spano and continues his productive teaching philosophy. Gary Dahl is a contracted staff arranger/recording artist for Mel Bay Publications, Inc. Mr. Dahl's accordion arrangements are marketed in the U.S.A., Canada and internationally.

---

For best results, the violin switch should be tuned wet (vibrato tuning, also known as musette tuning or French tuning). This switch is only used **alone**; **do not** combine with the bassoon reed or the piccolo reed because it will sound like an orchestra out of tune.

# Joue Contre Joue

**(Tango Chanté)**

**By Jacques Plante**
**By Louis Ferrari**
**Arr. by Gary Dahl**

1. 3.
2. 4.
B. S.
B. S.
M
7
d
7
rit..
1. Repeat
2. D.S. al
rit.
Freely, (no beat)
rit..
23
tr
7
Ending Cadenza
rit.
mp

# Cara Al Cielo

By Don Diego & Julio Falcom
Arr. by Gary Dahl

To di Tango

M
7
cresc.
f
p
1.
2.
D. S.
fin

# El Choclo

**By A. G. Villoldo**
**French Score by Andre Trichot - Marc Provance**
**Arr. by Gary Dahl**

**Tango**

8va 2nd Time
cresc.
decresc.
Loco
D. S. al Fine

# J'ai Pleuré Sur Tes Pas

By Roland Tessier
By Jacque-Simonot
Arr. by Gary Dahl

poco a poco
8va
Refrain
f
M
d
7

1.
Loco
D. S.
2.

# Tango Du Souvenir

By René Denoncin
Arr. by Gary Dahl

7
M
7
7
M
B. S.
M
M
M

M
1.
to Next Strain
2.
Fine
Couplet
d
8va
D. S.

# Soir de Pluie

Syam et Viaud
By Alstone & S. Bessière
Arr. by Gary Dahl

M' de Tango

Refrain

7
7
7
7
1.
2.
D. S.

# As De Copas

## (Tango Romance)

By M. Feijoo
Arr. by Gary Dahl

mf
cresc.
7
f
M

8va
Trio
Loco
D. S. al
Trio
7
M
d
D. S. al
f

# J'ai Gardé Ta Photo

Authors: Pierre Havet
Pierre Guitton

Composers:
By Jack Ledru &
René Denoncin
Arr. by Gary Dahl

To di Tango

Refrain
M
d
1.
2.
D. S.

# La Paloma

Marc Provance

Luis Coroma d'après
S. De Yradier
Arr. by Gary Dahl

7
M
M
7
M
7
7
D. S. al

# Tango Gitano

**Fernand Bonifay**
**Arr. by Gary Dahl**

B. S.
B. S.
7
7
7

Loco
7
8va
D. S. al
d
3
2
B. S.
Loco
3
M

*This page has been left blank to avoid awkward page turns*

# Tangorama

By R. Mendizabal
Arr. By Gary Dahl

M
7
d
1.
2.
D. S.

# Insaisissable

Hubert Ithier
By R. Denoncin
Arr. by Gary Dahl

**To di Tango**

2.
M
d
7
1.
2.
D. S. al
B. S.

# Maïa

**Louis Poterat**
**Guy Luypaerts**
**Arr. by Gary Dahl**

**M' de Rumba**

1.
2.
7
M
d

1.
2.
D. S.

# Téléphonez-Moi Chérie

**Maria Veldi**
**By J. Ledru & R. Denoncin**
**Arr. by Gary Dahl**

**Slow Tango**

M
7
d
M
Couplet
M
Loco
rit.
D. S. al

# Si Tu Reviens

Saint Giniez
By Tiarko Richepin
Arr. by Gary Dahl

**Tango moderato**

M
7
M
7
M
7
1.
2.
M
7
D. S.

# Sacré Tango

Maurice Capez
By René Denoncin
Arr. by Gary Dahl

M
M
D. S. al
M

# Le Tango De La Mélancolie

Jean Loup Dabadie
By Alain Goraguer
Arr. by Gary Dahl

Refrains

7
M
d
1.
2.
D. S.

# Tango Pour Madame

By T. Muréna &
A. Verchuren
Arr. by Gary Dahl

simile
B. S.
M
B. S.
simile
M

1.
2.
D. S.
M
f
7
8va
Loco
simile

# Simple Tango

By A. Verchuren & T. Muréna
Arr. by Gary Dahl

Trio
1.
2.
D. S. al Trio
D. S. al

# Ta Jalousie

JL Dabadie

By G. Jouannest
Arr. by Gary Dahl

M
1.
2.
D. S.

# Le Tango Des Mariniers

P. Carrel
By E. Prud'homme
Arr. by Gary Dahl

**To di Tango**

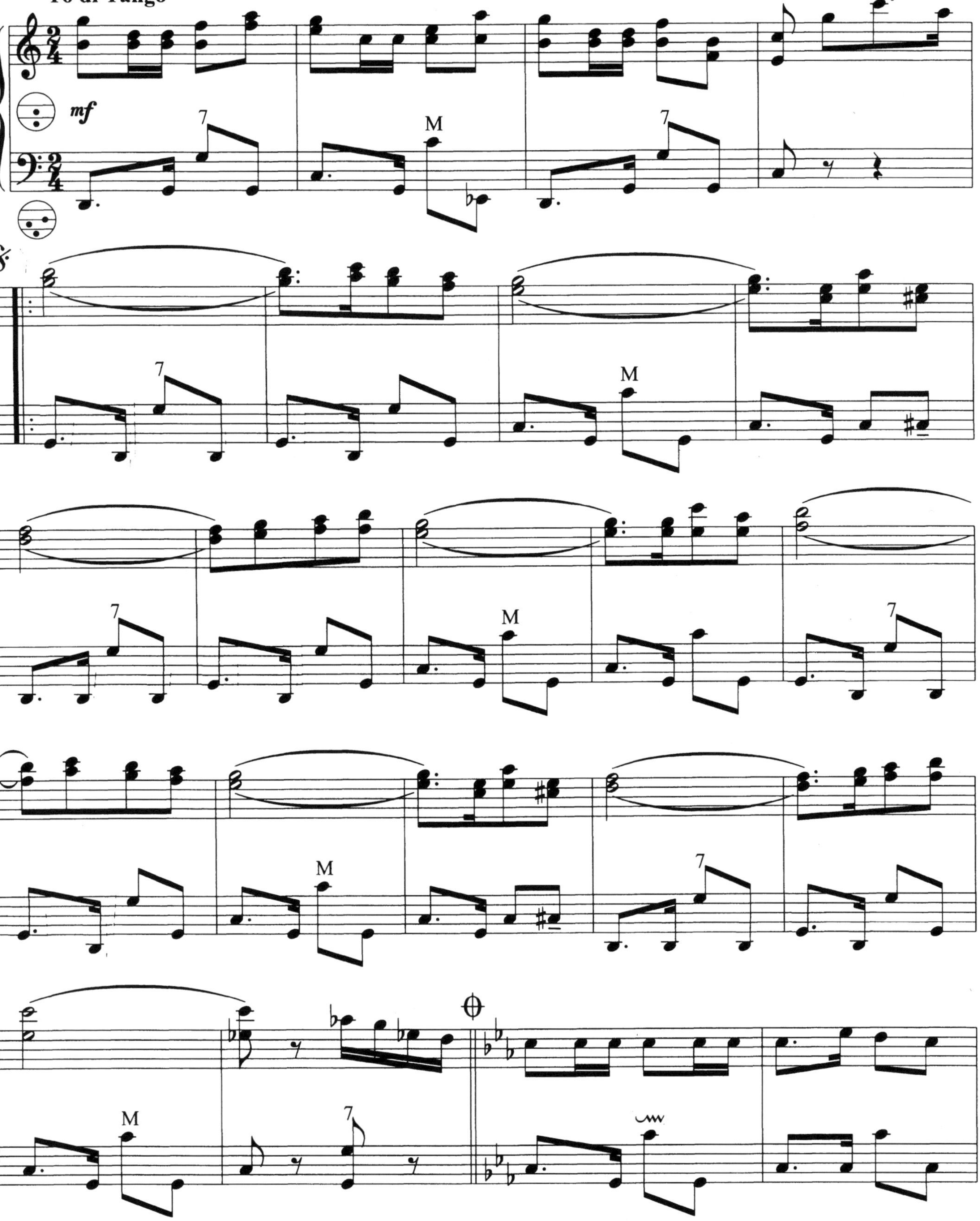

7
M
7
7
7
D. S. al

# Sensual
## (Tango)

**Hubert Ithier**
**By G. Gomez**
**Arr. by Gary Dahl**

7
M
d
M
d
7
M
1.
7
7
Loco
2.
D. S.
D. S. S. al

# La Madone D'amour

**(Tango Chanté)**

**Jean Pys**
**Gene Sandy**
**Claude Barẽs**
**To di Tango**

**By Théo Lecomte**
**Arr. by Gary Dahl**

2.
M
7
D. S. al Ⓐ to Ⓐ
Ⓐ

7
M
D.S. al Ⓐ to Ⓐ then ⊕ to ⊕

# Tango – Musette

R. Chabrier

Jo Moutet and
André Verchuren
Arr. by Gary Dahl

**To Tango**

M
7
1.
2.
D. S. al
f

# Ma Rose D'Alsace

Georges Coulonges

By R. Trabucco & M. Denoux
Arr. by Gary Dahl

**To di Tango**

M
2.
M
M
7
f
B. S.
fine
Couplet
mf
B. S.
D. S. al fine

# Tango – Maison

By André Verchuren &
Georges Ghesten
Arr. by Gary Dahl

fine
d
7
D. S. al fine

*This page has been left blank to avoid awkward page turns*

# Le Tango Argentin

**(Tango Danse)**

**By R. Desmoulins**
**Arr. by Gary Dahl**

**FL Bénech**

Refrain
rit.
7
M
D. S. al fine
Fine

# Un Tango D'autrefois

By Jo Privat & R. Duchesne
Arr. by Gary Dahl

Henri Jacques Dupuy

M
d
7
M
M
7
Couplet
7
7
7
M
7
8va
7
M
D. S. al
Fine

# Baisse un peu L'Abat-Jour

**Marcel DePmas**
**By Henri Bourtayre**
**Arr. by Gary Dahl**

M
d
M
7
M
7
7
M
7
M
7
7
1.
2.
D. S.

# Une Simple Carte Postale

Guy Bertret
Roger Desbois

By R. Denoncin
Arr. by Gary Dahl

Refrain
1.
2.
D. S.

# Aïe, Aïe, Tango

René Denoncin

C. Sauvage
By Pia del Moro
Arr. by Gary Dahl

1.
2.
7
M
d
D. S. al

# Pour Sûr

## Qu'est - C'que Tu Dis?
## (Tango Chanté)

Jean Rafa
Bourvil

By Emile Prud' Homme
Arr. by Gary Dahl

7
M
d
1.
2.
D. S.

# Le Temps D'un Tango

Christian Jollet
Guy Bertret

Armand Canfora
& Emile Decotty
Arr. by Gary Dahl

d
7
M
B. S.
D. S. al

# Tango Fleur Bleue

**Henri Contet**

**Armandino and Llanos Malendo**
**Arr. by Gary Dahl.**

7
M
d
8va

# Passion Madrileñe

## (Paso Doble)

By Abel & Bruno Lorenzoni
Arr. by Gary Dahl

Tempo di Paso Doble

Loco

7
7
M
7
7
M
m
7
M
7
7
M
7
1.
D. S.
2.
M